Printed in the United States of America

First Printing, 2020

ISBN 978-0-578-67018-8

Paradigm Shift
438 Gap View Dr.
Charleston, WV 25306

www.paradigmshiftbooks.com

fromcraigjackson@gmail.com

This little book is very powerful. If you wire
its concepts into your brain you will see an
amazing world you never knew existed.
You will see a world where all your dreams
come true.

How do you wire your brain?

You wire your brain by making brain cell
(neuron) connections.

You can do that by reading this book AT
LEAST once a day. You will be amazed by
the results.

Your brain was wired by your parents and
society by the time you were age seven,
mostly with limited beliefs. You are not
your brain. You can rewire your brain, make
new neural connections, and experience an
incredible world you can't see right now.

This book is not meant to be read it is meant
to be experienced and not just once but
daily. The pictures and statements in this
book are purposely combined to rewire your
brain. To accomplish this, you MUST read
the book AT LEAST once daily.

Believe it or not, until the 90s scientists didn't even think the brain was changeable. It was believed that after your youth your brain patterns were set and there was nothing you could do about it. Now we know that assumption was completely wrong.

The brain can rewire itself and they even have a name for it – neuroplasticity.

We think we are seeing everything around us. We are only seeing a very minute bit. What we see is determined by what we believe. Many are taught to believe many things which limit what they can see and therefore do and be.

This is why we created *50 Things You Needed To Hear As A Child*. We want you to experience the incredible power that is in each one of us. The power to create your world any way you wish.

This book will rewire your brain to see that. Children look to parents and other authority figures for security in an unfamiliar world. This, in turn, causes neural pathways to develop in patterns like the parent or authority figure. Therefore, children, for the most part, develop the same beliefs as their parents. Most live out their entire life and never question beliefs accepted as a child.

The pictures and statements in this book are purposely combined to rewire your brain.

As a child, we live in a world of miracles and magic. As we become adults the world loses its astonishment. As we interact more and more with the harshness of society the miracles and magic begin to fade. They do not have to.

It should be the exact opposite. The magic should increase but we were not told as a child how to keep the magic alive. Read (experience) **50 Things You Needed To Hear As A Child** to learn how to find the magic so many have lost.

You live in a world that has been programmed in fear. It is hard to escape because almost everyone you interact with and yourself has become a part of this world. It is hard to see a way out.

From childhood on this is the only world almost everyone knows. We are so easily influenced as a child that we can't see it does not have to be this way. Each generation brings the next into this fearful world blinded to the fact there is a way out. So, the next generation accepts that this is the way it must be.

It is a vicious cycle. We can put an end to the cycle and replace it with a world of kindness, gratitude, and love.

Get ready for an incredible blend of empowering life-changing statements and amazing photos. Read the book at least once daily. If you can do this for a week you will start seeing changes.

Everything is
energy.

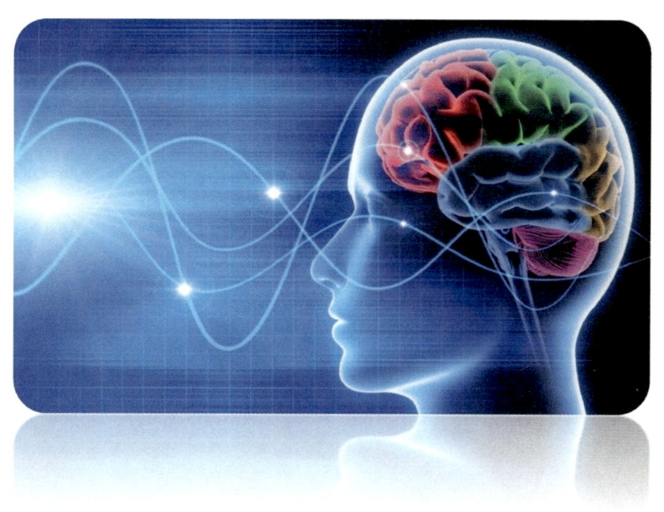

Just like televisions and telephones convert energy into sights and sounds, your brain converts energy into the sights and sounds of your reality.

Most of your beliefs were given to you by your parents (or at least the culture you were born into) before you were age 7. You never really questioned them.

QUESTION
EVERYTHING!

Everything and everyone are one. But that
does not mean you are not unique. You are
like a wave in the ocean. You are the
individual wave but you are also the entire
ocean. Everything you do affects everyone
and everything.

There is a database of the collective unconscious. We all share all knowledge. If one person knows it, be assured that information is available to you.

While you are always free to pull from the collective database of knowledge it is also your responsibility to add to it.

You are here to create. You are here to create your world in any way you want.

To create, use your imagination.
Picture anything you want in your
mind and add emotion. Hold that for
just a minute or two each day. It is that
simple.

There is nothing you
cannot do be or have.

Even after this life, you are still creating. You are creating infinite creations for all eternity.

Keep gratitude in your heart
and it will shield you from
the problems of the world.

Never force your point of view on
anyone. It won't work for them.
Love them for who they are and
for the unique gift they bring.

When you hear that voice in your head that says it is not going to happen... that voice is lying to you.

What others say about you
is not a reflection of you it
is a reflection of their world.
As you are a reflection of
your world.

All of your dreams lie on the other side of your fears.

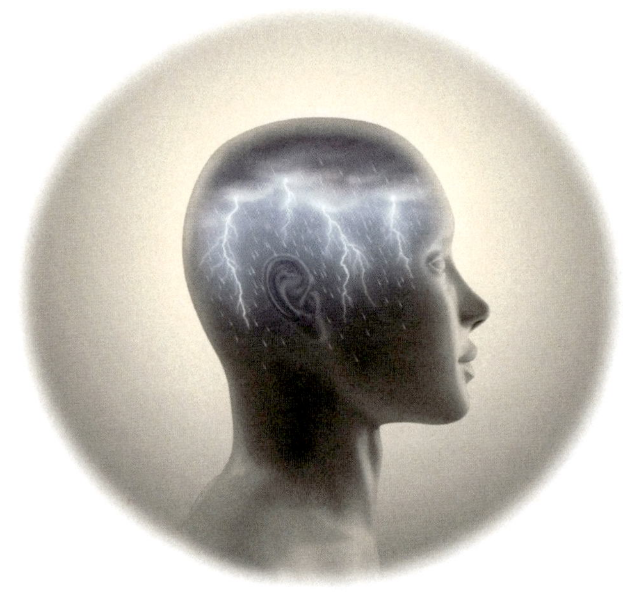

All your troubles are
just a storm within your
mind.

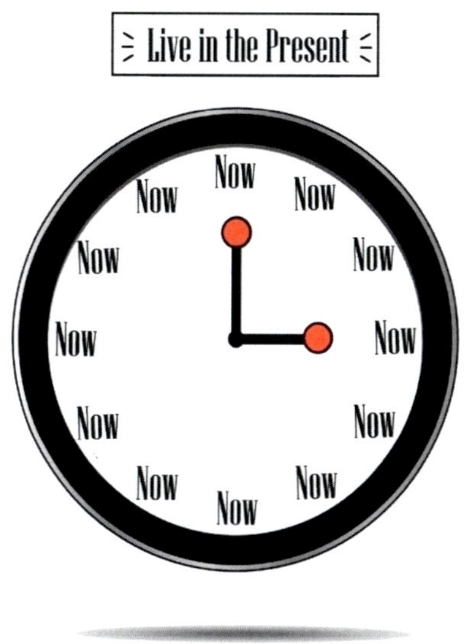

Past and future are just constructions of your brain. All there is... is NOW.

Do not let your
past limit your
future.

This world is just a
shadow of a greater
reality.

Any time you want to see your true beliefs just take a look at the circumstances of your life.

Stop trying to decide who is to blame and just decide you are going to be the one to fix it.

Silence your mind to
access Infinite
Intelligence.

On your journey through life, before you arrive at your destination you will find yourself at places you did not expect to be...but you will find your way. You will arrive.

Money is just a form of energy. It is
not good or evil. Money is a multiplier.
It magnifies one's personality. It makes
the bad worse and the good great.

Almost everyone is
possessed by their ego.

You can have what you
want if you can learn to get
your ego out of the way.

Detach yourself from
the things
you want.

Decide what you want
then let the universe open
the doors for you.

Stop making
excuses.

Want to know your future? What emotion are you feeling right now?

You are not your brain. You are
not your mind. You are not your
thoughts. You are not the voice in
your head. You are the observer
of the voice.

You are here to present
the world with a
present.

We have yet to even
imagine what we are
capable of.

Everyone sees the world differently. Your brain is bombarded by 10 million bits of information per second, you only process 40 bits. Your brain filters the other millions of bits through your beliefs. You see what you believe.

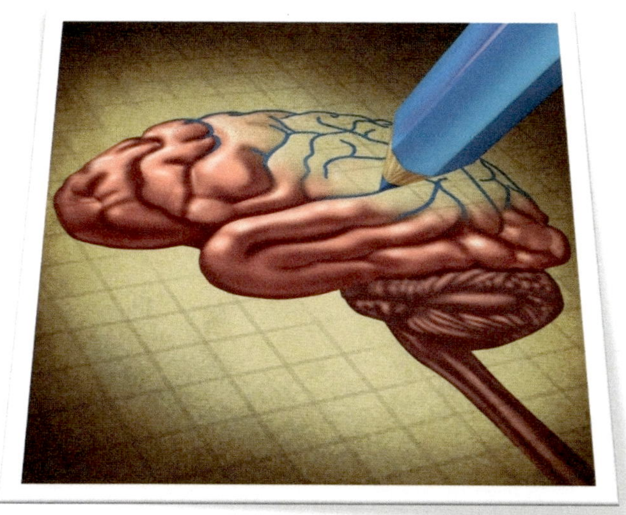

When you start to believe, your brain actually begins to rewire (rewrite) itself and you start to see things that have always been there you just couldn't see before.

Everyone needs help and everyone can help someone. This world would completely change if everyone helped just one person.

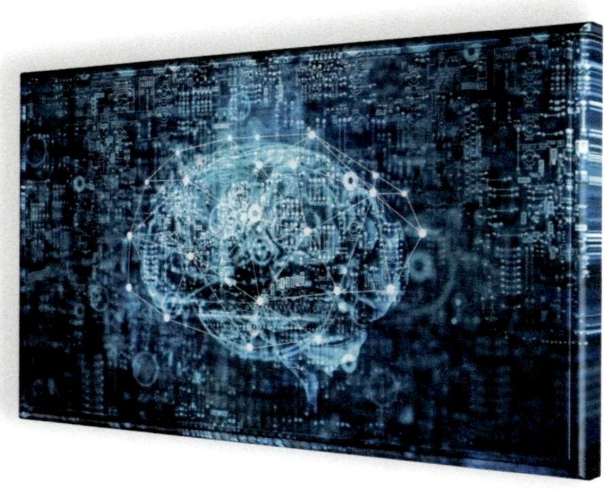

Just like any computer can be programmed to perform a task, your brain can learn to perform any task. Your brain is much more powerful.

You choose your
talents.

Once you truly make up
your mind to do something
the universe instantly sets
things in motion to help
you.

Do not follow the crowd.
Never let the negative
majority influence you.

You may have to
disappoint some people
to be true to yourself.

Your mind will come up with ideas that make sense but keep you from getting what you want. Your mind keeps you trapped.

There is no such thing as
scarcity. There is an
abundance of anything
you want.

Give to those who can't see the
abundance.

Do something new every day. See the world.

No one can see things from your perspective. The world needs your point of view.

Just start. Like GPS the universe will guide you and tell you if you make a wrong turn. But like GPS you must start to be guided.

It is never, not meant to be. If you
don't have what you want, it is
because you are not doing what you
need to do.

Change comes in
a single
moment.

If you read this
book every day
you will see
amazing changes
in your life.

Made in the USA
Monee, IL
16 April 2020